Schochler Primary School

_____of_____

THE NEW FOOD GUIDE PYRAMID

Grains

by Emily K. Green

BELLWETHER MEDIA • MINNEAPOLIS, MN

BLASTOFF!
2
READERS

Note to Librarians, Teachers, and Parents:

Blastoff! Readers are carefully developed by literacy experts and combine standards-based content with developmentally appropriate text.

Level 1 provides the most support through repetition of high-frequency words, light text, predictable sentence patterns, and strong visual support.

Level 2 offers early readers a bit more challenge through varied simple sentences, increased text load, and less repetition of high-frequency words.

Level 3 advances early-fluent readers toward fluency through increased text and concept load, less reliance on visuals, longer sentences, and more literary language.

Whichever book is right for your reader, Blastoff! Readers are the perfect books to build confidence and encourage a love of reading that will last a lifetime!

This edition first published in 2007 by Bellwether Media.

No part of this publication may be reproduced in whole or in part without written permission of the publisher. For information regarding permission, write to Bellwether Media Inc., Attention: Permissions Department, Post Office Box 1C, Minnetonka, MN 55345-9998.

Library of Congress Cataloging-in-Publication Data
Green, Emily K., 1966–
  Grains / by Emily K. Green.
    p. cm. — (Blastoff! readers) (New food guide pyramid)
Summary: "A basic introduction to the health benefits of grains. Intended for kindergarten through third grade students."
  Includes bibliographical references and index.
  ISBN-10: 1-60014-003-3 (hardcover : alk. paper)
  ISBN-13: 978-1-60014-003-7 (hardcover : alk. paper)
  1. Grain in human nutrition—Juvenile literature. 2. Nutrition—Juvenile literature. I. Title. II. Series.

  QP144.G73G74 2007
  613.2—dc22   2006000407

Text copyright © 2007 by Bellwether Media.
Printed in the United States of America.

Table of Contents

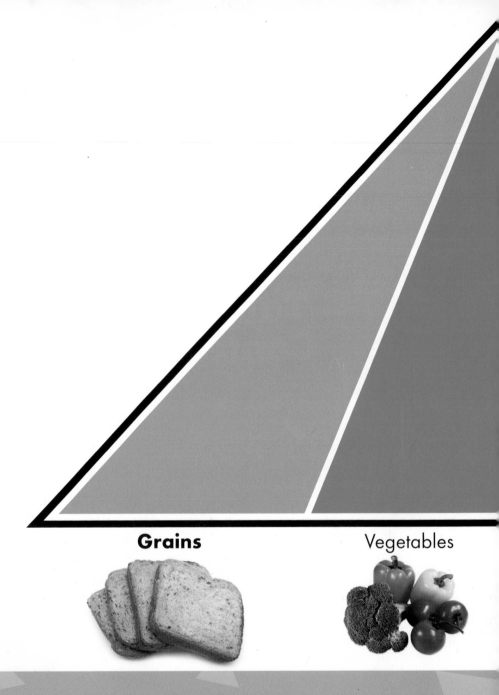

Grains

Vegetables

The **food guide pyramid** can help you choose healthy foods.

The Food Guide Pyramid

Fruits   Oils   Milk   Meat and Beans

Each color stripe stands for a food group. The orange stripe is for grains.

Bread is in the grains group.

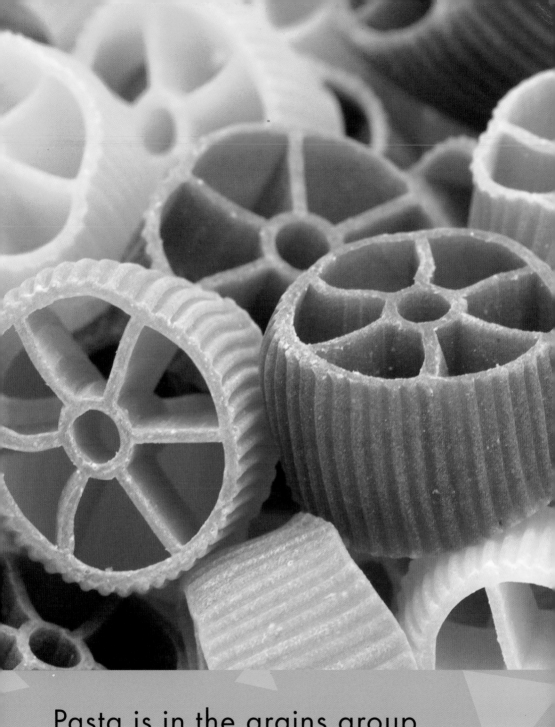

Pasta is in the grains group.

Grains are the seeds of **cereal plants**. Wheat is a cereal plant.

Rice is a cereal plant.

Foods made from the whole seed are called **whole grain** foods.

Whole grain foods are healthy for you.

Whole grains have **fiber**.

Fiber helps food move through your body.

Whole grains have **vitamin B**.

14

Vitamin B gives you **energy** to play and think.

Kids should eat about six **servings** of grains each day.

One slice of bread is one serving. Choose whole grain bread for a sandwich.

Eat a bowl of whole grain cereal for breakfast.

Make sure you eat grains
every day. Grains are great
for your body.

How Much Should A Kid Eat Each Day?

Vegetables
2½ cups

Grains
6 servings

Fruits
1½ cups

Oils
5 teaspoons

Milk, Yogurt, and Cheese
3 cups

Meat and Beans
1-2 servings

Glossary

cereal plant—a kind of plant with a seed that you can eat; wheat, rice, and barley are some kinds of cereal plants.

energy—the power to move

fiber—the part of a plant that stays whole when it moves through your body

food guide pyramid—a chart showing the kinds and amounts of foods you should eat each day

serving—the amount of a food group that you eat at one time

vitamin B—a part of some foods that helps your body make the best use of the healthy foods you eat

whole grains—grains that are made from the whole seed of the cereal plant

To Learn More

AT THE LIBRARY

Dooley, Norah and Peter J. Thornton. *Everybody Bakes Bread*. Minneapolis, Minn.: Carolrhoda Picture Books, 1996.

Gershator, David and Phillis. *Bread Is for Eating*. New York: Holt, 1995.

Rockwell, Lizzy. *Good Enough to Eat: A Kid's Guide to Food and Nutrition*. New York: HarperCollins, 1999.

Spilsbury, Louise. *Rice*. Chicago: Heinemann, 2001.

ON THE WEB

Learning more about healthy eating is as easy as 1, 2, 3.

1. Go to www.factsurfer.com

2. Enter "healthy eating" into search box.

3. Click the "Surf" button and you will see a list of related web sites.

With factsurfer.com, finding more information is just a click away.

Index